She Plays Basketball

By Trudy Becker

level
2
little blue
readers

www.littlebluehousebooks.com

Little Blue House is distributed by North Star Editions:
sales@northstareditions.com | 888-417-0195

Produced for Little Blue House by Red Line Editorial.

Photographs ©: Shutterstock Images, cover, 11, 12, 14–15, 21, 23, 24 (top left), 24 (bottom right); iStockphoto, 4, 7, 9, 16, 19, 24 (top right), 24 (bottom left)

Library of Congress Control Number: 2022910473

ISBN
978-1-64619-708-8 (hardcover)
978-1-64619-740-8 (paperback)
978-1-64619-800-9 (ebook pdf)
978-1-64619-772-9 (hosted ebook)

Printed in the United States of America
Mankato, MN
012023

About the Author

Trudy Becker lives in Minneapolis, Minnesota. She likes exploring new places and loves anything involving books.

Table of Contents

Getting Ready

I play basketball.

I love game days.

I put on my uniform.

I wear shorts and a jersey.

I tie my basketball shoes.

They have rubber

bottoms.

That helps me jump high.

I get my basketball too.

I put it in my bag.

I am ready to play.

hoop

At the Court

Games are at the basketball court.

The court has two hoops.

My coach helps the team.

It is time to play.

coach

In the Game

The whistle blows to start each game.

I dribble the ball.

It bounces up and down.

I stop.

I pass the ball.

Sometimes I am open.

I take a shot.

The ball flies toward
the hoop.

I make a basket!

My team gets two points.

I love basketball.

Glossary

basket

jersey

dribble

whistle

Index